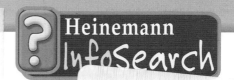

Heinemann
InfoSearch

Earth's Precious Resources

Minerals

A resource our world depends on

Heinemann
LIBRARY

Ian Graham

www.heinemann.co.uk/library

Visit our website to find out more information about **Heinemann Library** books.

To order:
☎ Phone 44 (0) 1865 888066
▤ Send a fax to 44 (0) 1865 314091
🖥 Visit the Heinemann Bookshop at www.heinemann.co.uk/library to browse our catalogue and order online.

First published in Great Britain by Heinemann Library, Halley Court, Jordan Hill, Oxford OX2 8EJ, part of Harcourt Education.
Heinemann is a registered trademark of Harcourt Education Ltd.

Editorial: Andrew Farrow and Dan Nunn
Design: David Poole and Paul Myerscough
Picture Research: Melissa Allison and Andrea Sadler
Production: Duncan Gilbert

Originated by Ambassador Litho Ltd
Printed in China by WKT Company Limited

ISBN 0 431 11552 4 (hardback)
08 07 06 05 04
10 9 8 7 6 5 4 3 2 1

ISBN 0 431 11560 5 (paperback)
09 08 07 06 05
10 9 8 7 6 5 4 3 2 1

British Library Cataloguing in Publication Data

Graham, Ian
Minerals: a resource our world depends on. – (Earth's precious resources)
1. Minerals – Juvenile literature 2. Mineral industries–Juvenile literature
I. Title
553
A full catalogue record for this book is available from the British Library.

Acknowledgements

The publishers would like to thank the following for permission to reproduce photographs: Corbis pp. **5 bottom**, 21 (Tom Bean), **27 bottom** (Michael Pole); Ecoscene pp. **5 top** (Papilio Neil Miller), **7 bottom** (Tony Page), **9 top** (Anthony Cooper), **12** (Joel

Cover photograph reproduced with permission of Corbis/First Light.

Every effort has been made to contact copyright holders of any material reproduced in this book. Any omissions will be rectified in subsequent printings if notice is given to the publishers.

The paper used to print this book comes from sustainable resources.

Contents

Any words appearing in the text in bold, **like this**, are explained in the Glossary.

What are minerals?

Minerals are natural resources that are found in the ground. They are the materials that rocks are made of. All minerals are made of **crystals**, like grains of salt squashed together. Some minerals, such as quartz and diamonds, sparkle, while many others look like plain rock and soil.

Most minerals are made from two or more substances combined. Many minerals contain a metal. Some of the metals found in minerals are also found in the ground on their own, not combined with any other substances. These metals are minerals too. They include gold, silver, copper and tin.

How are minerals formed?

Some minerals are formed when **molten** rock cools down and becomes solid. As the rock cools, the mineral crystals form in it. These are called primary minerals. Quartz and feldspar are examples of primary minerals. Other minerals are formed later, when rock is changed in some way, perhaps by

All the metals and **gemstones** we need are **mined** or **quarried** from the ground.

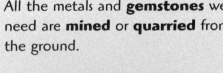

great heat or by being squashed very hard or by the effect of the weather. These minerals are called secondary minerals. Kaolinite, a mineral found in china clay, is an example of a secondary mineral.

Are minerals useful?

Minerals are very useful. Many minerals contain metals and other substances that are used to make things. Rocks that contain the most useful minerals are also called **ores**. A metal called aluminium comes from an ore called bauxite. Lots of other ores have names that end with '-ite' too.

Bauxite is mined because it contains the metal aluminium.

Did you know?

Coal, oil and natural gas are not minerals, because they come from living things. Even so, they are often called minerals or mineral fuels, because they are useful materials that are **extracted** from the ground.

What are minerals used for?

Almost everything around you contains minerals or materials that come from minerals. The latest electronic gadgets, airliners, cars and skyscrapers could not be made without minerals.

How are minerals used in buildings?

Big buildings start off with a steel frame. Steel is made from iron, a metal that comes from minerals such as haematite. The floors are made from concrete, which is made from limestone, a rock that contains minerals such as calcite and dolomite. Water is carried around the building inside pipes made from copper, which comes from minerals such as cuprite. The windows are made from glass, which is made from minerals that contain **silica**.

How do fireworks use minerals?

Minerals are what makes fireworks noisy and colourful. Aluminium powder produces the flashes and bangs. Iron

Ships are made from iron and steel, which come from minerals.

filings help to make golden sparks. Copper makes blue colours, barium makes green, sodium makes yellow and strontium makes red.

How are minerals used in jewellery?

Some of the most beautiful minerals are **gemstones**, which are used to make jewellery. They are **crystals** that form in places where the crushing weight of the rock above and very high temperatures change the rock. These minerals include diamonds, rubies, sapphires, emeralds, opals and garnets.

Minerals give fireworks their bright colours.

Did you know?

Some minerals are not what they seem. A mineral called iron pyrite is often mistaken for gold. Because of this, it is also known as Fool's Gold!

The most expensive jewellery is made from mineral gemstones such as diamonds and rubies. This ruby is worth about £8 million (US$15 million).

What amount of minerals do we use?

In a modern developed country, each person uses all of these minerals during his or her lifetime:

- about 40 grams (1.5 ounces) of gold
- 420 kilograms (925 pounds) of lead
- 380 kilograms (837 pounds) of zinc
- 730 kilograms (1610 pounds) of copper
- 1.6 tonnes of aluminium
- 10 tonnes of clay
- 13 tonnes of salt
- 15 tonnes of iron
- 770 tonnes of rock, stone, sand, **gravel** and cement
- 22.5 tonnes of other minerals and metals.

They are needed for generating electricity, providing warmth and making many other things.

Do living things need minerals?

Minerals are needed by plants and animals for growth and good health. The water plants draw up from the soil contains **dissolved** minerals. Animals get minerals by eating plants.

Minerals provide many of the things you will need in your lifetime, for example metal to make cars and materials used to build houses.

The human body contains up to about 3 kilograms (6.5 pounds) of minerals. You need the right amounts of about twenty minerals to stay healthy. The most important minerals our food gives us are calcium, phosphorus, magnesium, iron, iodine, sodium, potassium and zinc.

We get the minerals our body needs from our food and drink.

What do minerals do in your body?

Calcium, magnesium and phosphorus strengthen your bones and teeth. Sodium and potassium help your body's cells to work properly. Iron helps the blood to collect oxygen from your lungs and carry it around your body. Other animals use minerals in the same way.

Did you know?

Your body can actually make tiny amounts of a few minerals. One of them, called hydroxylapatite, is found in your bones and teeth.

CASE STUDY:
Sears Tower, Chicago, USA

Sears Tower in Chicago, USA, was the tallest building in the world when it opened in 1973. It stands 443 metres (1453 feet) tall and weighs more than 202,000 tonnes. The tower's framework was built from 77,000 tonnes of steel – enough to build 50,000 cars. It also contains enough concrete to build an eight-lane motorway 8 kilometres (5 miles) long.

The building's 110 floors, where 11,000 people work, are connected by about 70,000 kilometres (43,000 miles) of telephone cable made from copper – enough to go round the world 1.75 times. The outside of the building is covered with aluminium and windows tinted dark with bronze metal. All of these materials came from minerals.

Sears Tower in Chicago, USA, contains hundreds of thousands of tonnes of materials from minerals.

Where do minerals occur?

If you dig a deep enough hole in the ground, you will always find rock at the bottom. There is rock everywhere under the ground. This is the Earth's **crust**. Rock is made from minerals, so minerals are found all over the world.

Are all minerals found everywhere?

Minerals are not spread evenly everywhere. Some minerals are found concentrated in pockets or layers. A layer of one mineral running through rock is also called a seam.

The most common mineral in the Earth's crust is feldspar. The next most common is quartz. Minerals containing precious metals such as gold, silver and platinum are harder to find. These metals are very valuable, because they are so rare. Only about 195,000 tonnes of gold and 1.7 million tonnes of silver have been found in the whole of human history.

Rock sometimes forms in layers called strata. A layer of rock that is especially rich in one or more minerals is also called a seam.

How many minerals are there?

There are more than 3000 different minerals. Only about 100 of them make up most of the rocks on Earth. Most of these are made of only eight **elements** – oxygen, silicon, aluminium, iron, calcium, sodium, potassium and magnesium.

Are there minerals under the sea?

Minerals are found everywhere in the Earth's crust – under the land and under the sea. Minerals also come from the sea itself. Seawater contains bromine, lithium, boron and magnesium. Salt is made by heating seawater to boil off the water and leave the salt behind. Minerals are also found on the seabed. Large areas are covered with little lumps, called nodules. These contain a metal called manganese.

Most **sand** is made from **silica**, which contains the elements silicon and oxygen.

How are minerals found?

The search for minerals begins with photographs of the ground taken from aircraft and **satellites** in space. **Geologists** use these photographs to draw maps of the different types of rocks on the Earth's surface. The maps give clues about where certain minerals might be found. Small patches of one type of rock might mean there is more of the same rock, and the minerals it contains, underground. Geologists also try to work out how the land formed, because this can give clues about which minerals the rock might contain.

As well as looking at the rocks and testing them, there are ways of finding some minerals by using **magnetism**, **gravity**, electricity and **radiation**.

Photographs taken from a satellite show large areas of land at once.

Magnetism

Some minerals are magnetic. If they occur at or near the ground surface, instruments called magnetometers can detect their magnetism and show where they are.

Gravity

A large amount of a very heavy mineral can make the Earth's gravity pull more strongly near them. Instruments that measure the strength of gravity can pinpoint these minerals.

Electricity

Electricity flows better through some minerals than others. Measuring how well electricity flows through the ground gives geologists information about which minerals may lie underground.

Radiation

Some minerals give out **particles** of energy, called radiation. When geologists find this radiation, they know they have found minerals containing **radioactive elements** such as uranium.

Geologists test rocks to find out which minerals they contain.

How are minerals extracted?

Minerals are **extracted** from the ground by digging them out. Digging for minerals is also called **mining**. If minerals are near the surface, the ground above them is scraped away and a shallow pit dug to reach them. This is called open-cast mining. Minerals deeper underground are reached by digging shafts (passageways) down to them.

How are minerals dug out?

Some mineral-bearing rock can be dug out of the ground using a mechanical shovel. If the rock is very hard, it has to be broken into pieces by explosions before it is dug out. Some of the machines used in mining are the biggest in the world. There are giant mechanical shovels that can scoop up 100 tonnes of rock at a time. The shovels then load enormous trucks that can carry up to 363 tonnes of rock each.

Rock is shattered by explosions to make it easier to dig out.

What is panning?

It is possible to find gold without having to dig it out of the ground. If a river cuts through rock that contains gold, the water may wash out some of the gold. The heavy gold sinks to the bottom of the river. It can be found by panning. Water is swirled around a shallow pan with some river **sand** in it. The lighter sand is washed out while the heavy gold stays in the pan. Panning was a popular way of finding gold in the 1800s, but it is rarely used today because it only produces very small amounts of gold.

This goldminer was photographed panning for gold in California, USA, in 1890.

Did you know?

One of the world's deepest mines is the Western Deep Levels Gold Mine in South Africa. The deepest part is more than 3580 metres (11,745 feet) below the ground. There are plans to dig 5 kilometres (3 miles) below ground. This will be known as the Western Ultra Deep Levels.

What are the problems of deep mining?

Deep mining is very dangerous. Deep mines are hot and stuffy, and the ground can move. They have to be fitted with electric lights so that the miners can see to work and air has to be pumped down the mine so that the miners can breathe.

Deep mining is hot, dusty work.

Shifting ground

The Earth's surface is made from plates of rock that move. In places where the edges of the plates rub against each other, earthquakes are common. The ground may shake thousands of times a day. Most of these movements are so small they go unnoticed, but any movement of the ground inside a mine can spell danger.

Bursting rocks

The deepest mines can suffer from a problem called rock-burst. The huge weight of rock above, pressing down, can squeeze the rock at the bottom of the mine so hard that pieces fly out of the mine's walls.

As the miners cut into the rock, the roof has to be propped up to stop it from collapsing.

17

Hot rocks

The centre of the Earth is very hot, so the deeper a mine is, the hotter it is. At a depth of nearly 4 kilometres (2.5 miles), the rock is at a temperature of more than 60 °C (140 °F). It is impossible for miners to work in such a hot place, so the mine has to be cooled. Cooling down a mine is very expensive, so the deepest mines are dug for only the most valuable minerals, such as gold.

Did you know?

The centre of the Earth is made from iron, nickel and other valuable metals, but it cannot be mined because it is as hot as the surface of the Sun, 6000 °C (10,830 °F). You would also have to dig a mine more than 6300 kilometres (3900 miles) deep to reach it!

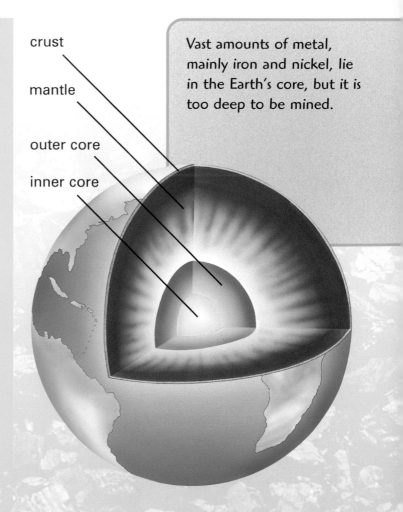

crust

mantle

outer core

inner core

Vast amounts of metal, mainly iron and nickel, lie in the Earth's core, but it is too deep to be mined.

CASE STUDY:
Bingham Canyon Copper Mine

The Bingham Canyon copper **mine** near Salt Lake City in Utah, USA, is one of the biggest holes ever dug in the ground. It measures 4 kilometres (2.5 miles) across and more than a kilometre (over half a mile) deep.

Mining began there in the 1860s, when people found lead, zinc, gold and silver **ores** there. Today, more than 170 million tonnes of rock is dug out every year, producing about 57 million tonnes of ore. Each tonne of ore produces only about 5 kilograms of pure copper. Alogether, the mine produces about 300,000 tonnes of copper, 100 tonnes of silver and 14 tonnes of gold every year.

The Bingham Canyon mine has been producing copper and other metals for about 140 years.

19

How are minerals processed?

Rock is **processed** to separate the most useful minerals from the rest of the rock. The processes used are crushing and grinding. Then the minerals are processed to **extract** useful materials from them. The processes used to do this are smelting and refining.

Why is the rock crushed first?

Crushing the rock produces a fine powder that is easier to separate into useful minerals and waste rock. Trucks bring the rock to crushers. They break the big chunks of rock into smaller pieces. Then these are ground down to a powder by tumbling them around with hundreds of steel balls inside spinning drums. These 'ball mills' produce a fine powder like very fine sand.

Rock is crushed to a powder to separate the minerals it contains.

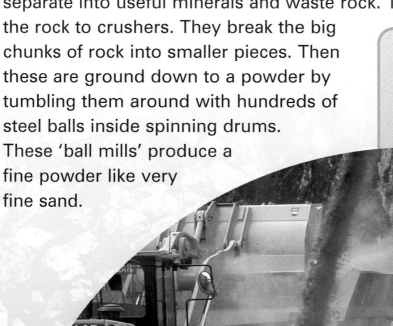

How are the minerals separated?

Some minerals are heavier than others. Letting the powdered rock slide across shaking tables can make heavier minerals slide off in one direction while the lighter waste rock goes off in another direction. This is called **gravity** separation. Some minerals are **magnetic**, so they can be picked out by **magnets**.

How is water used in minerals processing?

Powdered rock is mixed with water and then air is blown through the water to make bubbles. Some of the minerals stick to the bubbles and float to the surface, where they are skimmed off. This is called flotation separation.

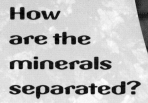

Some minerals and the metals they contain are magnetic. This magnet has been used to pick up a pile of iron filings.

Did you know?

Magnetic iron ore is also called lodestone.

What is smelting?

Once the minerals have been separated, the next step is to extract useful materials from them. Metals are extracted from **ores** by smelting. An ore is heated to a high temperature in a furnace. Other materials added to the furnace combine with the ore. They are chosen so that they split up the ore into the metal plus a waste material, called slag. The **molten** metal runs out of the furnace.

How is iron smelted?

Iron ore contains iron and oxygen. Iron is extracted from the ore by heating the ore to 1600 °C (2912 °F) with limestone and charcoal or coke (a kind of charcoal made from coal). Iron made in this way is called pig iron.

Minerals are smelted in a furnace to extract the metal they contain.

Why is iron made into steel?

Pig iron is not pure iron. It contains carbon, which makes the iron break easily. Pig iron is made stronger by taking out some of the carbon. Oxygen is blown through molten pig iron in a furnace. The oxygen combines with carbon in the pig iron and makes gases. The gases bubble out, taking the carbon with them. The metal produced in this way is called steel.

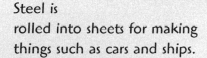

Steel is rolled into sheets for making things such as cars and ships.

A metal combined with another metal, or carbon, is called an alloy. Steel is an alloy of iron and carbon. Brass is an alloy of copper and zinc. Bronze is an alloy of copper and tin.

How are gemstones processed?

Natural **gemstones** look like pieces of dull glass. They are processed by cutting and grinding. First, they are cut into smaller gemstones with better shapes. Then flat areas called facets are made all over each stone. The facets act as mirrors, reflecting light. They give a cut gemstone its sparkle.

A well-cut diamond sparkles brightly.

CASE STUDY:
The Cullinan diamond

The world's biggest diamond was found in South Africa in 1905. It was named after Sir Thomas Cullinan, the mine's owner. Diamonds are weighed in carats. A carat is equal to 0.2 grams. The Cullinan diamond weighed 3106 carats, or about 620 grams (22 ounces). It was given to the British king, Edward VII. It was then cut into more than 100 diamonds. The biggest is the Star of Africa, or Cullinan I. This became part of the Royal Sceptre in the British Crown Jewels. The second largest diamond, called Cullinan II or the Second Star of Africa, was set in the British Imperial State Crown.

The biggest diamond in the British Royal Sceptre is the Star of Africa, which was cut from the Cullinan diamond.

Did you know?

The Koh-i-noor (a Persian phrase meaning 'mountain of light') diamond was owned by emperors of India from the 14th century. It was presented to Queen Victoria in 1850. Later, it was set in the crown worn by King George VI's queen at the coronation in 1937.

How are minerals transported?

Minerals have to be transported from where they are found to where they are processed. Then, the metals **extracted** from the minerals are transported all over the world to be made into things. Most minerals and metals are heavy and they usually need to be transported in large quantities, so big powerful vehicles are needed to move them.

Which vehicles transport minerals?

Minerals are transported mainly by trucks, trains and ships. Only the most precious metals and **gemstones**, such as gold and diamonds, are valuable enough to transport by air.

Did you know?

About 50 billion tonnes of **ore** are mined every year and have to be transported. That's enough rock to fill a hole that is 1 metre (about 3 feet) deep and the size of Switzerland.

Ore carrier ships like the ones here are also called bulk carriers.

CASE STUDY:
The Liebherr T282 dump-truck

The Liebherr T282 dump-truck is one of the biggest trucks in the world. Its job is to haul as much rock as possible as fast as possible out of **mines** and **quarries**.

It is far too big to travel on ordinary roads. It is about four times the length and five times the width of a family car. It is so big that it has to be taken to the place where it is needed in pieces and built there. Even when it is empty, the Liebherr T282 weighs more than 200 tonnes. With a full load of rock on board, it can weigh up to 560 tonnes.

The Liebherr T282 dump-truck is so big that the driver has to climb up a ladder to get into the cab.

How can minerals affect the environment?

Extracting minerals from the ground can damage the environment. Open-cast mines scar the landscape. **Mining** and mineral-**processing** can create huge spoil (waste material) heaps. Water running through mine workings and waste heaps can pollute nearby rivers and lakes. The waste materials produced when minerals are processed can also be dangerous to plants and animals.

Are some minerals more dangerous than others?

The most dangerous minerals are those that are **radioactive**. Just being near a radioactive **element** can be dangerous. **Radiation** can kill living cells or damage them. If cells that produce babies are damaged, newborn babies can be harmed.

Spoil heaps are the piles of waste rock and soil left over after minerals have been extracted.

CASE STUDY:
Chernobyl, 1986

The worst **radiation** accident in history happened near the city of Chernobyl in Ukraine in 1986, when part of a **nuclear power station** exploded. The explosion threw **radioactive particles** up into the air. They were carried away by the wind and blew across several countries. Thousands of people who lived close to the power station had to leave their homes. About 30 people died at the time of the explosion. At least another 8000 people have died since then from illnesses caused by the radiation. Some farm animals more than 3000 kilometres (1860 miles) away were affected by radioactive particles from Chernobyl. The particles had been blown by the wind and landed on the grass they ate. This meant the animals themselves became too radioactive for people to eat!

The damaged part of the Chernobyl power station was covered with concrete to stop more radiation from escaping.

Will minerals ever run out?

Nearly all the minerals we use today come from only the top 1000 metres (3300 feet) of the Earth's **crust**. If these minerals begin to run out, **geologists** will explore the next 1000 metres below that and then the next 1000 metres. The Earth's crust is up to 70 kilometres (43 miles) thick, so we have a long way to go! However, the deeper we have to go to find minerals, the more expensive it is to **mine** them. We can make the minerals we are mining now last longer by **recycling** them.

Where else could minerals come from?

So far, there has been very little mining underneath the sea. This may be done in the future, although it could have a huge effect on the environment and habitats. Further into the future, if minerals are in very short supply, it could be worth mining them on the Moon and bringing them back to Earth.

In the future, some of our minerals might come from the Moon.

Glossary

crust rock that forms the surface of the Earth

crystal material made from particles that form patterns. These patterns repeat themselves over and over again, making shapes with flat surfaces.

dissolved finely broken up within a liquid

element substance that cannot be split up into simpler substances. About 93 elements are found in nature and others have been made by scientists. Elements are made from particles called atoms.

extract to take out or obtain one substance from another

gemstones minerals that are highly valued, because they are so beautiful and rare. Gemstones include diamonds, rubies and sapphires.

geologist scientist who studies rocks and minerals

gravel pieces of rock that are very small but that are bigger than grains of sand

gravity force that pulls everything towards the Earth. Everything has its own force of gravity, but large objects such as stars, planets and moons have the strongest force of gravity because they are so big.

magnet material that pulls some metals, mainly iron and steel, towards it from a distance

magnetism/magnetic effect of a magnet

mine/mining digging into the ground to reach valuable materials such as minerals

molten melted, liquid form

nuclear power station building where electricity is made using energy from atoms – the smallest particles of an element. When uranium atoms are split apart inside a nuclear power station, they give out heat that is used to change water into steam. The steam drives machines, called generators, that make electricity.

ore mineral from which a metal, or metals, can be extracted

particle tiny piece

process to change a material by a series of actions or treatments

quarry hole in the ground where building materials such as stone or gravel are dug out

radiation particles and energy given out by radioactive elements such as uranium

radioactive giving out radiation

recycling collecting materials that have been used at least once already and using them again

sand loose particles of rock no bigger than about 2 mm across

satellite small object that orbits around a larger object, such as a spacecraft going around the Earth

silica substance containing silicon and oxygen joined together, found in many rocks and minerals; also called silicon dioxide

Find out more

Books

Heinemann Library's *Rocks and Minerals* series, Melissa Stewart (Heinemann Library, 2002)

Collins Wild Guide: Rocks and Minerals, Adrian Jones (Collins, 2000)

DK Eyewitness Books: Rocks and Minerals, R. F. Symes (Dorling Kindersley, 2003)

Philip's Minerals: Rocks and Fossils, W. R. Hamilton, A. R. Woolley and A. C. Bishop (Philip's, 2001)

Usborne Spotter's Guides: Rocks and Minerals, A. R. Woolley (Usborne Publishing, 2000)

Websites

www.mii.org
Information about minerals from the Mineral Information Institute.

www.idahoptv.org/dialogue4kids/season3/rocks/facts.html
Information about rocks and minerals from Idaho Public Television.

http://walrus.wr.usgs.gov/ask-a-geologist/
A website for asking a geologist questions.

www.mining-technology.com/projects/bingham
Information about the Bingham Canyon ore mine.

Disclaimer

Index